The Jewish Riddle Collection
A Yiddle's Riddle

Shapolsky Publishers, Inc.
New York

For additional information contact:
Shapolsky Publishers, Inc.
136 West 22nd Street,
New York, NY 10011
(212) 633-2022

First Edition
9 8 7 6 5 4 3 2 1

Library of Congress Cataloging-in-Publication Data

Brenner, Reeve Robert
The Jewish Riddle Collection: A Yiddle's Riddle

ISBN 0-933503-38-5

Printed and bound by Graficromo s.a., Cordoba, Spain

Dedicated to the grandchildren of Abe and Eva Brenner and of Rabbi Eli and Sonia Rosman:

>>*Neeva Liat Brenner*
>>*Nurete Leor Brenner*
>>*Noga Libi Brenner*

>>*Keith Elliot Reich*
>>*Leslie Brooke Reich*
>>*Jaime Meredith Reich Amivam*
>>*Avi Amiram*

>>*Gregory Seth Zuckerman*
>>*Ezra Wyatt Zuckerman*
>>*Shara Orly Zuckerman*

>>*Robyn Lynn Roth*
>>*Elana Gail Schrader*
>>*Stuart Neil Schrader*
>>*Steve Roth*

The sturdiest yet links in the chain of our people's continuity.

TABLE OF CONTENTS

ACKNOWLEDGMENT

This page has been set aside for the usual acknowledgments due to all those who contributed to this book. However they all pleaded with the author not to mention their names for fear of public humiliation. I will therefore acknowledge that their help wasn't worth much anyway judging from the quality of some of these Jewish clinkers.

Trifling, trivial; slight, slender, light, flimsy, frothy, idle; puerile &c. (*foolish*) 499; airy, shallow; weak &c. 160; powerless &c. 158; frivolous, petty, niggling; peddling, piddling, fribbling, fribble, inane, ridiculous, farcical; finical, finicking *or* finicky *or* finikin, mincing, fiddle-faddle [*colloq.*], namby-pamby, wishy-washy [*colloq.*], milk and water, insipid.

Int. No Matter! pish! tush! pshaw! pugh! pooh, -pooh! fudge! bosh! humbug! fiddlestick, -end! fiddledeedee! never mind! *n'importe!* [*F.*]; what signifies! what matter! what boots it! what of that! what's the odds! a fig for! stuff! nonsense! stuff and nonsense!

***magno conatu magnas nugas; le jeu ne vaut pas la chandelle; elephantus non capit murem; tempete dans un verre d'eau;* "why beholdest thou the mote that is in thy brother's eye?" [*Bible*]; "very trifles comfort, because very trifles grieve us" [*Pascal*]; "Come gentlemen, we sit too long on trifles" [*Pericles*]; "These little things are great to little men" [*Goldsmith*]; "Seeks painted trifles and fantastic toys, And eagerly pursues imaginary joys" [*Akenside*]; "Trifles unconsciously bias us for or against a person from the very beginning" [*Schopenhauer*].

Roget's Thesaurus; Vol. I (pg.264)

INTRODUCTION

The riddle is a liberating thing, a tool with which to pry open the lock on the Jewish psyche; particularly useful since the key has been inadvertantly locked inside. Moreover, the riddle may be characterized as a portal, because portals are nice. Nor has the word "portal" been especially overused of late — and it has a good ring to it (perfect from the pulpit, to let you in on a trade secret). Clearly, riddles *are* portals. Whether exiting or entering or merely passing through, there, eternally, is the riddle.

The classical Jewish riddle has a great history about which you will read elsewhere. The reader may ask what makes the perfect Yiddle's Riddle? Clearly it should show great scholarly insights on multiple levels, exhibiting subtle historical and theological nuances while making one wince just short of seizure. This suggests diligent application of the art of delivery. This art will be the topic of the next profound work of this series, eagerly awaited to be sure, entitled *How to Deliver a Yiddle's Riddle.*

In that work the notable distinction between the concepts dreck and drivel as independent variables will be carefully scrutinized from the perspective of the Halacha of the Riddle. The point will be made that the term "Useless Riddle" is an oxymoronic redundancy, by definition, inherent in itself, that is intrinsically, essentially if not existentially; i.e. fundamental to its nature — which is to say, basic as opposed to pish! tush! tut! pshaw! rot! etc. The category of "Tasteless Riddle" does not fall within these parameters, but, like the mitzvah itself, every riddle may yet have its day. We are not to judge in advance even the flattest and most tasteless riddles which have been gathered in this collection. We are, however, obligated by tradition to utter them frequently.

The author hastens to add that this important contribution to an unjustifiably neglected field of intellectual inquiry is by no means the definitive, final word on riddles. One has to admire the author's modesty.

Grounded in strict rabbinical authority, but also at the incalcuable cost of delaying the Messiah further still, the author has scrupulously avoided attributing authorship to many of these blatantly plagiarized scraps of worthless dreck so as not to reflect shame on these otherwise estimable members of the folk and faith who, in moments of passing weakness, first uttered them. The reader may think that the author, by this shameful devise, is attempting to bypass the obligation evolving upon a researcher of attribution by footnotes and texts, trusting and scheming that he can get away with it. Stop thinking that at once!

You may ask, "Why did you write this book under both your real name Reeve Robert Brenner and your pseudonym Reb Reeven?" One hardly expects to see, *lehavdil*, the pseudonym Mark Twain alongside his real name Samuel Clemens. Certainly not while he was still living. You may further ask: "Is it because you really did not want to be associated with such piffle, much less come forward as the author?" And you may be thinking with some sarcasm: "Don't tell me it took courage to admit to fathering this text, and that perhaps we should admire the fact that you have courageously taken full responsibility for these pages, coming forward to confess as much with your real name on the cover." The reader may also consider that the author wishes to be thought of as collecting and compiling these riddles while engaged in some other serious work, perhaps as a kind of therapy. DO think such thoughts.

By all logic this collection promises to sow the seeds of revulsion and discord, if not outright disharmony and dissension, in households everywhere. Caveat Emptor: An empty cavity is *The Jewish Riddle Collection*. And conversely, a Yiddle's Riddles makes for an empty cavity.

A RIDDLE: A POEM

How odd
of God
to choose
the Jews?

Oh no
it's not
God knows
what's what.

Is the news
so odd?
The Jews
chose God.

How odd
of Jews
who refuse
to choose.

Dear God
how odd
the Jew
is so few.

Reeve Robert Brenner
The Jewish Spectator
Sept. 1965

REJECTED SOLUTIONS TO A RIDDLE

Rejoice
the choice
annoys
the goys.

How odd
of Jews
to occupy
the pews.

It's odd
when God
is a riddle
to a Yiddle.

To a Yiddle
with a riddle
it's God
who's odd.

Give the Yiddle
a fiddle
he solved
the riddle.

It's the Id
In the Yid
that's odd
my God!

O Shut Up,
Reb Reeven!

ABOUT THE AUTHOR

Reb Reeven is the nom-de-embarrassment *(shem busha)* behind which Reeve Robert Brenner stands proud and tall in ducking responsibility for this book. In his intermittently serious mood swings, Reeve has published poetry, fiction, memoirs, responsa, and numerous essays on Jewish history and contemporary Jewish thought and Jewish Law. His study, *American Jewry and the Rise of Nazism* won the YIVO Award (1966).

His research on the theological effects of the Holocaust has received a number of prestigious international prizes and his book, *The Faith And Doubt of Holocaust Survivors* (Free Press, 1980) is considered the definitive study on the effects of the Holocaust and is a frequently cited reference in Philosophy, the Sociology of Religion as well as Holocaust Studies.

His biography is included in Who's Who in Poetry, Who's Who in Religion, Who's Who in Israel, and Who's Who in World Jewry.

An athlete of some considerable reputation, Reeve has, in connection with the International Year of the Disabled, invented a new sport, the first new ball playing sport in over half a century — and the second basketball sport. Bankshot Basketball is a TOTAL MIX, non-exclusionary sport, which is now being played in parks, recreation centers and sports complexes in more than 50 cities in the United States and Israel. Tournaments have been regularly featured on the major networks and in the press.

His sculptures, "Sportstructures," have been exhibited in several museums, including the Israel National Museum in Jerusalem, and the Museum of Modern Art in New York City.

Of Boro Park and yeshiva background, Rabbi Brenner was ordained in New York at the Hebrew Union College-Jewish Institute of Religion and is currently serving the Bethesda Jewish Congregation in Maryland as spiritual leader. He likes to refer to his congregation as "low synagogued, independent, full-equality, Polydox, Total Mix, intimate and intellectual; and possessing great-hearted tolerance of his feeble attempts at humor, bless-their-souls."

His hobby is raising endangered hatchling turtles and releasing them as adults to their original habitat.

His three daughters Neeva, Nurete and Noga have each in turn been running off to join the Israeli army from their home in Netanya, Israel for the avowed and loudly proclaimed purpose of "wrenching free finally from the pernicious grasp of their father's wretched riddles" or words to that effect - or other effect. And since their words were spoken in Hebrew, not their father's native tongue, very little effect indeed. They have not much looked back. They have, however, looked forward; and they have looked upon their father with compassion and love, much to their father's relief.

Why then, the reader may wish to ask, would anyone inflict these riddles on another, particularly one's family seeing that, from grimaces to threats of bodily damage, such hostility is evoked? Don't.

One must think rather of the tradition of the venerable blow across the cheeks administered by certain Chasidic Masters who would on occasion call upon the frask in pisk, undoubtedly influenced cross-culturally by the Zen Buddhist practice of a smart slap across the face of the true disciple at given intervals and for no apparent reason or observable act on the part of the student.

It may be of value to calibrate with exactitude precisely the point at which children raise whatever they're holding — and the kitchen is full of dangerous objects — and proceed to threaten their father with corporal punishment, technically known as *Makot Avot*, Blows to the Fathers, which will one day become a well known tractate of the Mishna. Then again, it may not.

It can be disclosed here that history begins with the riddle of antiquity: what first walks on four legs, then on two and lastly on three, whose answer **is not** "Man, I don't know;" then proceeds to Samson's stinger in a book not by his name and continues from there...

It may interest the reader to know that this publication is hardly the first which Reeve Robert Brenner has written by pseudonym. The scholarly inclined reader may wish to consult under various other names for other works by him: Yosef Hayim Brenner (I am in beard in photo), George Ade, Tolstoy, Ephraim Kishon, Robert Benchley, S.J. Perelman, The Oxford English Dictionary (OED), Mark Turidg and Franz Kafka.

It has been a well known secret for some time now that Reeve Robert Brenner writes under his own name but thinks under the names of Samuel Atlas, Eugene Borowitz, Herbert Brichto, Martin Cohen, Shaul Hareli, Julius Kravetz, Leon Liebreich, Harry Orlinsky, Paul M. Steinberg, John Tepfer, et al. To these great scholars and thinkers of our time, Reb Reeven was a darkness in their luminaries and a blackness in their light. They all in turn take full responsibility for their denial of their influence upon his life.

ABOUT THIS BOOK

Perhaps you'd think to ask, "How does this sophomoric collection of driveling riddles, devoid of humor the first time around, imbecilic jokes prancing about in question and answer tutus, plus some wisecracks and poorly planned puns, get to be published in the first place? And worse, end up in the hands of someone of my high calibre? Don't.

You have stumbled upon the single most important research project in the annals (with two `n's) of our people, the one volume of Jewish wisdom certain to last into the century after the next — not wishing the book's career less than the prescribed and venerable 120 years. "How," you may ask, "is this book — or if you would rather, 'collection,' of yours — even granted it's a kind of research — bad, I may add — to be taken as lasting and not trivial and frivolous?" Don't.

Also, bear in mind that except for the very good ones, I do not make up these riddles, only collect them.

Unfortunately, the best Jewish riddles of all time, past and future, have no place in this collection and will not be published here for obvious reasons. For example:

Q: What is the difference between a crucifixion and a circumcision?
A: In a crucifixion they throw the whole Jew away.

The reader will agree that this kind of humor has no place in this collection, and will not be published in these pages. Jewish American Princess riddles, on the other hand, constitute a special category to be found beginning on page 613.

Riddles which ask on which holiday do Jews eat in the dining room and smoke in the bathroom (the Sabbath) and on which do we smoke in the dining room and eat in the bathroom (Tisha b'Av) and on which do we smoke and eat in the bathroom (Yom Kippur) will never be printed in a volume of integrity such as this.

Another type of riddle which has no place in this collection is the riddle which asks, why do some Jews chant "Shma

Yisrael I deny Elohenu, I deny Echad;" and which, "Shma Yisrael I don't know Elohenu, I don't know Echad." Even those who cannot sing "I do know Elohenu," *do* know Yisrael; *do* know Echad. They can be at one with the people and know the people as one.

"Enough with the sermons, Rabbi," you may say. You may.

The first riddle I remember inventing was as a child of four. I was, at the time, in a neighbor's hallway in the Bronx, researching a little girl named Francine. And baseball was also on my mind, please believe. Another new discovery. I was just beginning my life-long passion for the game, and with my super Orthodox religious upbringing beginning to take hold, my thought at that indelicate moment was, "Could God pitch a ball so fast that He couldn't hit it?" I concluded He'd hit it out of the park, since the act of hitting followed in time sequence the act of pitching, the latter cancelled out by the former. And so, God could <u>not</u> pitch a ball so fast that He couldn't pounce on it. As good a pitcher as God is, He's a better batter, *baruch hashem*. But it occurred to me, I had found something God couldn't do, as I pictured Him winding up and throwing His best hard slider and reappearing instantly at the plate swinging with a Mighty Force. God, not connecting with the ball, was unthinkable. I wondered how far the ball would travel and I therefore refer the reader to the cover for the answer to the profoundest of riddles. I am certain the reader will feel comforted by this theological digression offered as a solution to one of the world's perennial conundrums.

You might feel ashamed to be wasting your time on something so trivial, trifling and frivolous as this. Don't. Consider that in this repository there is to be found much of the intellectually deepest, most penetratingly scholarly and enlightened insights of our folk. And your innermind and better self will agree that in these pages lies the ultimate in Jewish Profundity, which as far as the author is concerned, is a rather high form of profundity. And, bear in mind, that for Jews, identity precedes theology, folk comes before faith, belonging takes priority to believing, acts antecede obeisance, deeds supercede creeds and study overrides dogma. And if faith is to be held as admirable, doubt provides education. Judaism, therefore, proposes the priority of human experience and community considerations to any doctrine, theory or ideology, implying that this research and so forth ... oops, lost my concentration. Instead, take the first pitch and hit to right. Sorry about that.

You may alternatively wonder, "What of the question which asks, `In what sense can you argue that the historical stages of theological progression which were represented by the patriarch Abraham's rejection of human sacrifice in the Akedah, in favor of animal sacrifices, marking the birth of Judaism, developing through the substitution of the sacrificial cult with synagogue prayer, symbolized as sacrifice of the lips, correspond with the historical stages from the biblical, prophetic prewritten Toraic "open" period, through the written, "closed" period of reference to the text, to the modern idea of a God of history and of nature by way of the stage which offered the God of classical philosophy and mysticism, can be understood in such a way that future projections, if not predictability, may be forthcoming for the sake of the survival of the community?'" What?

This volume should also enable the reader to distinguish between a (mere) question and a (sublime) Yiddle's Riddle. The reader will observe at once that we have here proposed a distinction with a difference. Be mindful too that a question receives an answer, whereas a riddle requires a resolution. And from the Q and A process the reader may expect to learn something — which is clearly not the case for the R and R process — the violation of which would entail a serious infraction of the Jewish Halacha, which is one of the more authentic kinds of Halacha.

We were discussing earlier, shame and wasting good money buying a book such as this. The correct response might be "that's why Yom Kippur exists." Be mindful too that there is no concept in Judaism of a surrogate Messianic charismatic figure, and certainly not a god who offers himself to die for the sins of humanity," at which time I give you a swift boot to your rump, in the tradition of the Zen Buddhist Chasidim, and offer an hypothesis on Jewish religious thought explaining how the central motif of that great document "Ein Kelohenu" is upside down and is only itself inches away from nonsense. Which brings us to riddles. A place not one of you in your right mind would go without my guidance and direction. "But which of you is in a right mind anyway seeing you are already reading this preface about riddles," you might say. Don't. You would be overlooking the great insights of the folk "Aw, c'mon" you might say. Don't.

Every reader's mind has no doubt already leaped to the traditional Jewish prayerbook and to the hymn already referred to above, the Ein Keloheni, a prayer on every readers' lips, daily. But only a select warped few readers whose great wisdom and learning allows them best to appreciate the inspiration of one of the very most ancient unsolved riddles in the Jewish world of scholarship (which, by definition, implies it is greater than even the riddle of the sphinx) can understand:

Q. Who put the Ein Kelohenu question in the middle of its own solution?
A. Ameniac.

It would constitute a ritual of highest priority for you, the reader, to memorize the content of these pages so that when the opportunity arises you may demonstrate your riddles-skill by deliberately interjecting a particularly juicy and tasteless one into serious conversations and settings. A business meeting for example dealing with the future of your company is an especially appropriate context. Speaking slowly you ask:

Q. (i.e. R) Why does the shlemiel leave an empty glass on his night table alongside a full glass of water?
A. (i.e. R) The empty, in case he should wake up and <u>not</u> be thirsty.

You have made it clear to everyone in attendance that you have much to say worth listening to. A small, sly smile will begin to play on your face, proving that you don't take yourself too seriously. Then, ask in a soft voice, just above a whisper:

Q: What is the term for an uncircumcised Jewish child?
A: A girl.

You may be thinking, "Now I know how to make use of these riddles." Don't.

The notion that the riddle is a light, charming genre of the common man and woman, of amcha, as opposed to revolting and dreadful is to be resisted. This book will undoubtedly uphold and support that resistance and will expose the falsehood of any other assumption.

You might think at this point "The rabbi does go on a bit." Stop thinking that at once.

Instead, enter the portals of the Yiddle's Riddles. Welcome seekers of truth or other things.

One final word: One should never ask, "Would you like to hear a riddle?" Courtesy of this sort is bad form, and not in the tradition of the genre. One inflicts a riddle, remember. It is punitive by nature. Therefore, blaming the victim is entirely appropriate in this instance. If the riddler (the reader is to take note of this usage) can get away with it, go for it.

RIDDLES FOR THE SCHOLAR

1. Q. Why do Jews answer a question with a question?

2. Q. How do you tell a Jewish chromosome from a non-Jewish chromosome?

3. Q. What do they call an uncircumcised Jewish child?

4. Q. If one of your two chickens get sick, what do you do?

5. Q. When a Jew is confronted with two solutions, which does he choose?

6. Q. What is a Jewish slum in Italy called?

7. Q. Where is the majority of world Jewry found?

(Answers on next page)

ANSWERS

1. A. Why shouldn't Jews answer a question with a question?

2. A. By pulling down their genes.

3. A. A girl.

4. A. Kill the other one and make some chicken soup for the sick one.

5. A. Of two solutions, he chooses the third.

6. A. A Spaghetto.

7. A. I didn't know it was lost.

8.   Q. Why were the Jews elected the chosen people?

9.   Q. What happens when you bring three Jews together?

10.   Q. Why in Jewish tradition is the *Kallah* (bride) unlucky on her wedding day?

11.   Q. For what man alone does even the most orthodox Jew remove his *yalmulka?*

12.   Q. What is a Jewish telegram?

13.   Q. Can the eggs of an unkosher rooster be eaten by a religious Jew?

14.   Q. Why does a chicken cross the road?

15.   Q. Why is there a gate on all Jewish cemeteries?

(Answers on next page)

ANSWERS

8.   A. To spare others from always getting it in the neck.

9.   A. You have three Jews, four opinions and five synagogues.

10.   A. Because the *Husan* (groom) never turns out to be the best man.

11.   A. For his barber.

12.   A. Start worrying letter to follow.

13.   A. Yes, because a rooster does not lay eggs.

14.   A. Not to get to the other side but to escape from the *shochet* (ritual butcher).

15.   A. For order and crowd control. After the resurrection everyone would be rushing to get out and we wouldn't want anyone hurt.

16. Q. What are the Ten Commandments?

17. Q. What is black and white and red all over?

18. Q. When a Chinese or Japanese woman converts to Judaism, what is she called?

19. Q. And the coffee expert's demanding Jewish wife?

20. Q. What fruit should not be grown in a Jewish neighborhood?

21. Q. What are the three rings connected with a Jewish marriage?

22. Q. What was the name of the first disco-tec in Jewish history?

23. Q. What is the best diet for a Jewish husband?

(Answers on next page)

ANSWERS

16.   A. One more than the Nine Commandments.

17.   A. The *Torah* which is read all over the world.

18.   A. An Orieyenta.

19.   A. El Exeyenta.

20.   A. A Goyava.

21.   A. First the engagement ring, then the wedding ring, and finally the suffering.

22.   A. Let My People Go-Go.

23.   A. To eat only what his wife cooks.

24.   Q. What should you do when you discover your best friend is having an affair?

25.   Q. What religious beliefs are held by radical Jewish feminists?

26.   Q. Why did the child continue to draw a picture of God even after he was informed that nobody knows what He looks like?

27.   Q. What's a bad battle of wits?

28.   Q. If one is God, and two are the tablets of the covenant, and three are the patriachs, what are four and five?

29.   Q. What does a baby become after he's eight days old?

30.   Q. What is a Jewish optimist?

(Answers on next page)

ANSWERS

24. A. Help her find a really good caterer.

25. A. Not only is God dead, She is turning over in Her grave.

26. A. He figured now they'd know.

27. A. An argument among Moskowitz, Hymawitz and Itzkawitz.

28. A. Nine.

29. A. Nine days old.

30. A. One who, given world conditions, would be a pessimist if his
        neighbor hadn't already become one.

31.   Q. From which Jewish ritual object may a man learn how to treat his wife?

32.   Q. What is inscribed on a Jewish homosexual's tombstone?

33.   Q. According to Jewish law what is the first thing a man must do when his doctor tells him he has but six months to live?

34.   Q. Why do Jewish women have cleaner minds than Jewish men?

35.   Q. What is a gastronomic Jew?

36.   Q. What is a cardiac Jew?

37.   Q. What is a revolving door Jew?

(Answers on next page)

ANSWERS

31. A. From the *Mezuzah*, because you should always kiss her when entering your home.

32. A. Gay in dred.

33. A. Find another doctor.

34. A. See how often they change them.

35. A. One whose Jewishness consists of eating bagels and lox.

36. A. One who feels Jewish in his heart.

37. A. One who is in on *Rosh Hashana* and out on *Yom Kippur*.

38. Q. For the Jewish scholar, what is worse than a learning disorder?

39. Q. How is a Jewish joke like Jewish history?

40. Q. What are the three words describing your talented, beautiful daughter who is still single?

41. Q. How do you know that the car ahead of you is driven by a *shadchan* (marriage broker)?

42. Q. What is a Jewish sadist?

43. Q. What is a Jewish masochist?

44. Q. Why does the *shlemiel* keep an empty glass as well as a full glass of water by his bed?

(Answers on next page)

ANSWERS

38.   A. A test-taking disorder.

39.   A. It is always being repeated.

40.   A. Picky, picky, picky.

41.   A. Because the bumper sticker reads: If you get any closer introduce yourself.

42.   A. One who would not visit his mother because she'd enjoy it too much.

43.   A. A Jewish mother who will not invite her son to visit because she knows how much she'd enjoy it.

44.   A. The empty glass is in case he should wake up and *not* be thirsty.

45. Q. Why did the Rabbi refuse to vary his lovemaking and why did he pick his nose?

46. Q. Why do Jewish divorces cost so much?

47. Q. Why do Jewish husbands die before their wives?

48. Q. What do you say when you bring your home-made chicken soup as a gift to your friend?

49. Q. What kind of world was it until Eve arrived?

50. Q. What was God's second mistake?

51. Q. How do we know that Moses and Herzl were really the same person?

(Answers on next page)

<u>ANSWERS</u>

45.   A. He was advised that if he didn't screw up and kept his nose clean, he'd enjoy a fine career.

46.   A. They're worth it.

47.   A. They prefer it that way.

48.   A. "God forbid you should need it."

49.   A. It was a man's world.

50.   A. A woman.

51.   A. Were they ever seen together?

52.   Q. Why should you not pray for immortality?

53.   Q. For essential information when moving into a new neighborhood, to which service in the Yellow Pages do you turn?

54.   Q. What is the proper term for doing something bad in a unique and creative way?

55.   Q. What is better than having all the answers?

56.   Q. Is life worth living?

57.   Q. What is faith?

58.   Q. How do you respond to an atheist who insists he can believe only in something he can understand?

(Answers on next page)

15

ANSWERS

52.   A.   It tends to go on forever!

53.   A.   Renta Yenta!

54.   A.   Original sin.

55.   A.   Knowing some of the questions!

56.   A.   That depends on the liver!

57.   A.   Believing in what you know isn't so.

58.   A.   "Oh, so that's what explains why you believe in nothing."

59. Q. How is Jewish ethics like art?

60. Q. Why did God make time?

61. Q. Why can't you have it all?

62. Q. What is the main point of Jewish philosophy?

63. Q. What is more costly than Jewish education?

64. Q. When we talk to God we are praying. What are we when God talks to us?

65. Q. What is a hypocrite?

66. Q. What is the new maxim of the airhead who inherits a vast Jewish library?

(Answers on next page)

ANSWERS

59.   A.   They both consist of drawing the line somewhere.

60.   A.   To keep it all from happening at once.

61.   A.   Where would you put it?

62.   A.   That there must be more to life than having everything.

63.   A.   Jewish ignorance.

64.   A.   Schizophrenic.

65.   A.   A hypocrite is a person who...but who isn't?

66.   A.   Heir today, Gaon tomorrow.

67. Q. What is the major problem with God having created everything out of nothing?

68. Q. What is the essence of Einstein's Theory of Relativity?

(Answers on next page)

ANSWERS

67. A. The nothingness shows through.

68. A. Time slows down when you are with your relatives.

RIDDLES FOR THE SCRIPTURALLY ILLITERATE

1.   Q. How do we know that baseball was on God's mind at the creation?

2.   Q. What was there before the Big Bang?

3.   Q. Why was man not created on the first day?

4.   Q. What did God do on the eighth day?

5.   Q. How do we know that Adam was a great athlete?

6.   Q. What time of day was Adam born?

(Answers on next page)

ANSWERS

1.   A. The bible teaches : IN THE BIG INNING GOD CREATED THE HEAVENS AND THE EARTH.

2.   A. God only knows.

3.   A. God knew that with his kibitzing man would have driven Him crazy all the rest of the week.

4.   A. He started answering complaints.

5.   A. He was first in the human race.

6.   A. A little before Eve.

7.   Q. Arriving at the Garden of Eden, what did the well-bred time traveller say to Eve?

8.   Q. What did Adam and Eve do after they were banished from Eden?

9.   Q. On what grounds did Cain plead for sympathy?

10.   Q. Why were Adam and Eve happily married?

11.   Q. But why did they have difficulty conversing?

12.   Q. Where did Noah strike the first nail he put in the ark?

13.   Q. All the animals came to Noah's ark in pairs except for which one?

14.   Q. Why was the rooster happiest in the Ark?

(Answers on next page)

ANSWERS

7.   A. "Miss, O Miss, might I suggest you avoid the fruit round these parts?"

8.   A. They raised Cain.

9.   A. On the grounds that he was dis-Abled.

10.   A. a) Adam didn't have to listen to his wife talking about the man she could have married.

           b) No mothers-in-law either.

11.   A. Because they had nobody to talk about.

12.   A. Right on its head.

13.   A. The worms. They came in apples.

14.   A. Because with one crow he could awaken the whole world.

15.   Q. Why couldn't the animals in the ark play cards during the forty boring days of rain?

16.   Q. What was the theme song on Noah's Ark?

17.   Q. After forty days, why did Noah want the rain to keep up?

18.   Q. What did the Animals say when they got off the Ark?

19.   Q. Who conducted services on the Ark?

20.   Q. On what did Noah stand when he landed on the mountain with his ark?

21.   Q. What was Noah's wife's nickname?

22.   Q. In the bible what twins are mentioned after Jacob and Esau?

(Answers on next page)

ANSWERS

15.   A. Noah was standing on the deck.

16.   A. Raindrops keep falling on my head.

17.   A. He was tired of it coming down.

18.   A. "Not a bad trip, but where's the beach?"

19.   A. The prayerie dog and the praying mantis.

20.   A. On his feet.

21.   A. Joan of Ark.

22.   A. First and Second Samuel.

23.   Q. What were Pharoah's daughter's first words, when she spotted a baby floating in the Nile?

24.   Q. How were the ancient Egyptians able to build the enormous pyramids?

25.   Q. What did the Red Sea say as the Israelites crossed through?

26.   Q. Why was Moses the greatest sinner?

27.   Q. In the bible, what time was it when Moses smashed the two tablets?

28.   Q. Who was the greatest actor in the Bible?

29.   Q. In which battle was King Saul slain?

(Answers on next page)

ANSWERS

23. A. She exclaimed, Holy Moses!

24. A. They took very few coffee breaks.

25. A. Not a thing, it just waved.

26. A. He alone broke all the Ten Commandments at once.

27. A. It was time for a new set.

28. A. Samson, he brought down the house.

29. A. His final one.

30.   Q. What did the weatherman say to King David?

31.   Q. The giant Goliath was so big, how many hard boiled eggs do you think he could eat on an empty stomach?

32.   Q. How did Solomon become the wisest man in the world?

33.   Q. Why was the patient depressed when his psychiatrist told him he was now cured?

34.   Q. What inspired Isaiah to a great career?

35.   Q. Why do we read the book on Jonah on the Day of Atonement, the holiest day of the Jewish year?

36.   Q. How did Jonah feel when he was swallowed by the giant fish?

(Answers on next page)

<u>ANSWERS</u>

30.   A. Hail King David, may you rain forever.

31.   A. One! After the first his stomach is no longer empty.

32.   A. He had so many wives behind the throne to guide him.

33.   A. Before his cure he was King Solomon, now he felt he was a nobody.

34.   A. It was the Prophet motive.

35.   A. Because it's a whale of a story and no fluke.

36.   A. Down in the mouth.

37. Q. Who was the greatest doctor in the Bible?

38. Q. How do we know that Moses was an expert at delegating authority?

39. Q. How do we know that Moses was a great team player?

40. Q. Name at least three references for constipation in the Bible.

41. Q. Who was the shortest man in the Bible?

42. Q. What was the period after the exodus called?

43. Q. What did Queen Esther do when she burped?

44. Q. Why was the author of the Bible so successful?

(Answers on next page)

ANSWERS

37.   A. Job, he had the most patience.

38.   A. The bible tells us he leaned on his staff.

39.   A. Whenever it was necessary he laid down a perfect sacrifice.

40.   A. Cain wasn't able, Balaam had trouble moving his ass, and Moses took two tablets.

41.   A. Knee-high Meyer.

42.   A. The days of whine and Moses.

43.   A. She issued a royal pardon.

44.   A. He was in the write business.

45. Q. What prevents God from sending another flood?

46. Q. What did God do when He finished creation?

47. Q. Why should you not pray that God will bless you as He did Abraham, Isaac and Jacob?

48. Q. Judging from the history of the world what can be said about Noah and the flood?

49. Q. What was the real reason Jesus was put to death?

50. Q. According to Jewish Law, when are contraceptives permissable?

(Answers on next page)

ANSWERS

45. A. The realization that the first one failed to accomplish its purpose.

46. A. He started working on an ambitious project.

47. A. Abraham was a wanderer, Isaac went blind and Jacob, lame.

48. A. It's a pity that Noah and his party didn't miss the boat.

49. A. Because he wouldn't become a Jewish doctor.

50. A. On every conceivable occasion.

RIDDLES ON JEWS AND OTHER CHARACTERS

1. Q. What is the name of the main boulevard through a *Hasidic* neighborhood?

2. Q. Why was the traditional Jewish father called a permissive parent?

3. Q. What does a Jewish actor become when he has a nose job?

4. Q. How did the Vatican bell sound after the Jewish repairman fixed it?

5. Q. What was the line of defense employed by the chutzpadik defendant who caused the death of his parents?

6. Q. How do we know that there are many Jews living in the North Pole?

7. Q. What did they call Sherlock Holmes' brother who worked in the garment district?

(Answers on next page)

ANSWERS

1. A. Rue de la Payyis.

2. A. He always permitted his children to work hard.

3. A. A thing of beauty and a goy forever.

4. A. Goyim, Goyim, Goyim.

5. A. He threw himself upon the mercy of the court on the grounds that he was an orphan.

6. A. Iceberg is hardly a Christian name.

7. A. Sherlock Holmes' ohmateh brother.

8. Q. Who is the cleverest husband in the world?

9. Q. What does your mother give you when you inform her of your plans to marry a man just like she did?

10. Q. How do you know that the widow who was left a million dollars really loved her departed husband?

11. Q. Why did the seriously ill sixty year old stock-broker know that his time was up even though he was relatively young?

12. Q. What period furniture did the newly rich Jewish lady seek to purchase for her new home?

13. Q. When does a lawyer's advice on health veto a doctor's?

14. Q. In the garment industry how do you know you're doing business with a gonif?

(Answers on next page)

ANSWERS

8.   A. The one who convinces his wife she'll look fat in a mink coat.

9.   A. Sympathy.

10.   A. Because she'd gladly give ten thousand dollars just to have him back.

11.   A. He figured if God could get him at sixty why should He wait until he hits eighty?

12.   A. The kind of furniture which when her friends see it they should drop dead, period.

13.   A. When, after an automobile accident, a doctor says you can walk but a lawyer says you can't.

14.   A. When the wool he pulls over your eyes isn't.

15.   Q. What does a furrier say to clients whose payments are in arrears?

16.   Q. Why couldn't Goldberg explain to the policeman that he was innocent?

17.   Q. When your business rivals on each side of your store put up seasons clearance signs, what sign should you erect?

18.   Q. Why did Abie consent to marry an ugly widow with a seventy-two room mansion?

19.   Q. When asked to lend twenty-dollars to the well known Schnorer, why did the rich man hand him a ten-dollar bill?

20.   Q. Why were the descendants of the Jewish immigrants more worthy than the descendants of the Mayflower generation?

21.   Q. Why do Jewish dentists enjoy treating their own wives?

(Answers on next page)

ANSWERS

15. A. No gelt, no pelt.

16. A. He was already handcuffed.

17. A. Main Entrance.

18. A. In a house of seventy-two rooms how much would he be seeing of her?

19. A. He reasoned this way we'll be even, we both lose ten dollars.

20. A. Because the immigration laws were much stricter for the Jewish immigrants than at the time of the Mayflower.

21. A. That is the only time they can tell them when to open and shut their mouths.

22.   Q. Why does the delicatessen employ midgets as waiters?

23.   Q. Why was she so happy about her husband's nervous breakdown?

24.   Q. What is a Psychiatrist?

25.   Q. What is a definition of a *shiksa*?

26.   Q. What is the Biblical method of teaching typing?

27.   Q. Who has the smartest grandchildren in the world?

28.   Q. If a man earns 500 dollars a week and his wife spends 1,000 what does he have?

29.   Q. Why is it easy for a Jewish wife to forgive and forget?

(Answers on next page)

ANSWERS

22.   A. They make the sandwiches look bigger.

23.   A. The doctor prescribed Miami for the cure.

24.   A. A Jewish doctor who can't stand the sight of blood.

25.   A. A woman who does her own housework.

26.   A. Seek And Thou Shalt Find.

27.   A. The same woman whose son-in-law wasn't good enough to marry her daughter.

28.   A. A nervous breakdown.

29.   A. Because she'll never forget what she forgave.

30.   Q. Why was the woman in the department store trying on a blouse blindfolded?

31.   Q. What motivated Henry Goldberg to become a multi-millionaire?

32.   Q. What does the first partner say to the second partner after being informed by him that they had been robbed?

33.   Q. How does Grandma introduce her two grandchildren?

34.   Q. What did the doctor instruct his patient who came to him complaining of developing a faulty memory?

35.   Q. Why was the clumsy young woman politely described as a cross between the Queen of Sheba and Camille?

36.   Q. If Finkelstein the peddler had all of Rothschild's money how would he be richer than Rothschild?

(Answers on next page)

ANSWERS

30.   A. It's supposed to be a surprise for her birthday.

31.   A. He wanted to see if there was an income his wife couldn't live beyond.

32.   A. Put it back.

33.   A. The lawyer is eight, the doctor is six.

34.   A. To pay his bill in advance.

35.   A. She was a *shlemiel*.

36.   A. He'd still do a little peddling on the side.

37. Q. Why did the perspective groom turn down the perspective bride, even though she looked like a picture?

38. Q. Why did the husband rush home to tell his wife the good news that the landlord raised the rent?

39. Q. Why did the businessman refuse to discuss his assets and profits with the Internal Revenue agent?

40. Q. Why was Sadie known as the best housekeeper?

41. Q. If a woman faints from the heat in Miami what must be done at once?

42. Q. Why did the Chinese Restaurant feature Italian Pizza as its Wednesday special?

(Answers on next page)

ANSWERS

37. A. He didn't care for Picasso.

38. A. Because now they didn't have to move to a more expensive apartment.

39. A. About those things he doesn't even tell his partner.

40. A. When her husband gets up in the middle of the night to go to the bathroom she makes his bed.

41. A. Remove her mink.

42. A. It was a Jewish neighborhood.

43.   Q. What Jewish couple living together for a decade can claim to be perfectly happy?

44.   Q. In a Jewish restaurant what is the Chef's surprise?

45.   Q. How is it that in Shapiro's delicatessen the Chinese waiters all speak *Yiddish?*

46.   Q. Why did the rich man refuse artificial respiration for his nearly drowned wife?

47.   Q. Why was Max more than willing to buy his wife the Jaguar she asked for?

48.   Q. What curse comes along with the Bloomstein diamond?

49.   Q. Why was Sam so forgiving at his wife's death-bed confession that she had been unfaithful?

50.   Q. Why was the mother unperturbed when the psychiatrist diagnosed her son as suffering from a prolonged Oedipus complex?

(Answers on next page)

ANSWERS

43. A. A Jewish mother and her ten year old son.

44. A. The surprise is being able to walk away from the table unassisted.

45. A. Sh! They think they're learning English.

46. A. He felt he was rich enough to afford the real thing.

47. A. One bite and she'd never ask for another expensive thing.

48. A. Mr. Bloomstein.

49. A. It was he who had poisoned her.

50. A. She thought it would get better so long as he loved his mother.

51. Q. Why did Sadie want the doctor to give her deceased husband an enema?

52. Q. How is it Molly was sporting an impressive diamond ring a week after her husband's burial?

53. Q. Why did Shapiro express the wish that his friend should live 120 years plus a few days?

54. Q. What were the patients first words after he was told he would be charged twice as much for the first doctor's visit as to subsequent visits.

55. Q. What were the three lines of defense employed by the defendant when he was sued for breaking a priceless vase?

56. Q. What did Rifka Silverman become when she joined the feminist movement?

(Answers on next page)

ANSWERS

51. A. It wouldn't hurt.

52. A. His last request had been that she buy a large stone in his memory.

53. A. He didn't want his friend to die suddenly.

54. A. Hi Doc! Good to see you again.

55. A. That he never had the vase, and that it was already broken when he received it, and that it was unbroken when he returned it.

56. A. She became Rifka Silverperson.

57.   Q. What do they call a cool beatnik who can't earn a living?

58.   Q. Why was little Abie so happy being chosen to play one of the Wise Men at a school Christmas play?

59.   Q. How does a neighborhood Yenta refer to herself?

60.   Q. Why did the Jewish statesman turn down the White House?

61.   Q. What are two things Jews know best?

62.   Q. How are *blintzes* the opposite of circumcision?

63.   Q. What is a Jewish relationship?

64.   Q. When do Jewish women become great housekeepers?

(Answers on next page)

ANSWERS

57. A. A Hep-schlep.

58. A. His grades were awful.

59. A. Telecommunications professional.

60. A. It would have cost a fortune in *mezuzot*.

61. A. Suffering and where to find great Chinese food!

62. A. Blintzes affirm your Jewish identity without pain.

63. A. That's what happens between a Jewish man and a Jewish woman who are waiting for someone better to come along!

64. A. After their divorce they invariably get to keep the house.

65. Q. What is a paranoid Jewish mother?

66. Q. What do they call a Jewish woman who has difficulty with calculations?

67. Q. What is the best husband a Jewish woman can have as she grows old?

68. Q. What is the most important thing in a relationship between a Jewish man and a Jewish woman?

69. Q. Why is it that some Jewish men cannot marry?

70. Q. How is a Jewish marriage like a bank account?

71. Q. Why does a Jewish parent never raise his hand to his children?

72. Q. What is the perfect gift for a middle-aged Jewish woman on her birthday?

(Answers on next page)

ANSWERS

65.   A. One who suspects people of trying to make her happy.

66.   A. A mother.

67.   A. An archaeologist.

68.   A. One of them should be good at taking orders!

69.   A. Some can't mate in captivity!

70.   A. You put in, you take out, you lose interest.

71.   A. Doing so leaves the mid-section unprotected.

72.   A. Not to be reminded of it.

73.   Q.   What is being hooked on Jewish LSD?

74.   Q.   Why did Benny want Meyer to convert to Christianity?

75.   Q.   When is it appropriate for a wife to divorce her husband for religious reasons?

76.   Q.   How is a Jewish marriage like a violin?

77.   Q.   What does the Jewish mother tell her son who asks to go outside to see an eclipse?

78.   Q.   On which day of a young Jewish man's life are the chances of getting a good job in the Soviet Union cut drastically?

79.   Q.   What is a Jewish wife's definition of enough?

(Answers on next page)

ANSWERS

73. A. When you can't get enough of Lox, Salami and Danish.

74. A. Because he wanted at least one Christian friend.

75. A. When she worships money and he doesn't have any.

76. A. When the music is over the strings are still attached.

77. A. "Alright, but don't get too close."

78. A. On the eighth.

79. A. Once.

80. Q. How do Jewish grandmothers make home movies?

81. Q. What is the most popular labor-saving device for a Jewish woman?

82. Q. Why is it that being a Jewish woman is so difficult?

83. Q. According to Jewish tradition what is the best way to keep one's vow?

84. Q. What is a Jewish mother's best revenge?

85. Q. What is the most dangerous food a Jewish man or woman can eat?

86. Q. How can you tell from a local book store if you're in a Jewish neighborhood?

87. Q. How are Jewish husbands like fire?

(Answers on next page)

ANSWERS

80.   A.   By editing out all the fun parts.

81.   A.   A husband with money.

82.   A.   Because it requires dealing with Jewish men.

83.   A.   By not giving it.

84.   A.   Living long enough to become a problem to her children.

85.   A.   Wedding Cake.

86.   A.   The cook books outsell the sex books; 3 to 1.

87.   A.   They go out if unattended.

88. Q. What is the happiest period of a Jewish man's life?

89. Q. When do Jewish couples seek divorce?

90. Q. What is the appropriate thing to tell the nasty Yenta who never has a nice word to say about any of her neighbors or friends?

91. Q. What's the best possible thing you can say about Jewish egotists?

(Answers on next page)

ANSWERS

88.   A.   Just after his first divorce.

89.   A.   When they run out of anniversary gift ideas.

90.   A.   Come sit next to me. Let's talk.

91.   A.   At least they don't talk about others.

RIDDLE ME A LITTLE

1.   Q. What looks like a box, smells like lox, and flies?

2.   Q. What looks like a beigel, smells like shmalz-herring, and crawls?

3.   Q. What is more dreadful than a man-eating shark in the aquarium?

4.   Q. From what planet in the solar system did the people of Israel originate?

5.   Q. What is the planet Mars red?

6.   Q. At Christmas, to whom is the nativity church in Bethlehem barred?

7.   Q. How does a Jew greet the Pope on Christmas?

(Answers on next page)

ANSWERS

1.   A. A flying lox-box.

2.   A. There's no such thing.

3.   A. A man eating herring on the bus.

4.   A. Jewpiter.

5.   A. It blushes at its ignorance of the Jewish question.

6.   A. To all Jews except one.

7.   A. The correct salutation is, Good Yontif, Pontiff.

8.   Q. What is a traditional Jewish Yuletide greeting?

9.   Q. Where can a *minyan* of Jews stand under one umbrella and not get wet?

10.   Q. When a Jewish boy falls into the water what is the first thing he must do?

11.   Q. When out fishing, what do you do if you get a Haddock?

12.   Q. What is the ultimate *Chutzpah?*

13.   Q. What do you call a Jewish elf?

14.   Q. What is a Jewish permanent wave, or a Jewish Afro called?

15.   Q. What do you call the Jewish dare-devil?

(Answers on next page)

ANSWERS

8.   A. Lend me a hundred dollars and you'll tide me over the week-end.

9.   A. Wherever it is not raining.

10.   A. He must get wet.

11.   A. Take an aspirin.

12.   A. Entering a revolving door behind someone and stepping out before him.

13.   A. A leprecohen.

14.   A. Izz-Frizz.

15.   A. Evil-Knish.

16.   Q. What happens when you eat Chinese Jewish food?

17.   Q. What is the difference between a Jew and a beigel?

18.   Q. What was the condition of the Jewish Physicians of History?

19.   Q. What is a wrench?

20.   Q. What is the difference between shillings and pence?

21.   Q. In *Yiddish*, what is the word beginning with "A " meaning prince?

22.   Q. What is a genius?

23.   Q. What is a Jewish intellectual called?

(Answers on next page)

ANSWERS

16.   A. An hour later you're hungry again but you still have heart-burn.

17.   A. Nothing, when they're both well bred.

18.   A. They were all well-healed.

19.   A. A Jewish resort with horses.

20.   A. You can walk down the street without shillings.

21.   A. A doctor.

22.   A. An average student with Jewish parents.

23.   A. A He-brow.

24.   Q. How do we know that the moon is more important than the sun?

25.   Q. How many seasons are there in the Jewish calendar?

26.   Q. Why is it plain foolishness to close the window when its cold outside?

27.   Q. The Guernsey cows and the Holstein cows say moo. Cross them and what are the results?

28.   Q. Why was it believed that a precious vase had been stolen in the course of a burglary?

29.   Q. When your father wants to discuss with you the facts of life, what do you answer?

30.   Q. What is a minor operation?

(Answers on next page)

ANSWERS

24.   A. The sun shines by day when its light out anyway. The moon shines by night when we really need it.

25.   A. Two: busy and slack.

26.   A. Because even after you close the window it still is cold outside.

27.   A. Goldstein cows that say nuu.

28.   A. The victim kept repeating, "Oy vase mer! Oy vase mer!"

29.   A. "Sure Dad, what would you like to know?"

30.   A. One which is performed on somebody else.

31. Q. In Jewish life how do we know that success is relative?

32. Q. What is the difference between karate and judo?

33. Q. Why is a Jewish attorney never attacked by a barracuda?

34. Q. What is the name of the sushi restaurant in the Jewish neighborhood?

35. Q. When is a Jewish fetus considered viable?

36. Q. How do you account for the Jewish drive for success?

37. Q. How many Jewish mothers does it take to change a light bulb?

38. Q. What is a Jewish Robin Hood?

39. Q. How do you keep a Yiddle's Riddles reader in suspense?

(Answers on next page)

ANSWERS

31.   A. The more success, the more relatives.

32.   A. One is a form of self defense, the other is what you use to make a bagel.

33.   A. Professional courtesy.

34.   A. So Sue Me.

35.   A. When it graduates medical school.

36.   A. It is the Id in the Yid.

37.   A. It's alright, I can sit in the dark.

38.   A. He steals from the rich and plants trees in Israel.

39.   A. If we provide the answer where's the suspense?

40. Q. What is the conclusive proof that God creates as a committee?

41. Q. What is love?

42. Q. What does a Jewish mother say about her short son?

43. Q. How does a riddle collector resemble someone who eats cherries?

44. Q. What do you give the man who has everything?

45. Q. What could be worse than writing these Yiddles Riddles?

46. Q. Why was the half-Spanish, half-Jewish soprano having trouble with her career?

(Answers on next page)

71

ANSWERS

40. A. The world.

41. A. Love is what happens to a Jewish man and a Jewish woman who haven't gotten to know each other yet!

42. A. So what if he's short, he can stand on his wallet!

43. A. He begins by chosing the best, but doesn't stop until he consumes even the rotten ones.

44. A. Penicillin.

45. A. Having to read them.

46. A. She never knew whether she was Carmen or goyim.

47. Q. What does the Jewish parrot shout?

48. Q. What did the Jewish cannibal say when his friend told him he hated his mother-in-law?

49. Q. Why are there no Soviet Jewish Cosmonauts?

50. Q. When are the two most appropriate occasions to eat chicken in a Jewish family?

51. Q. How do you circumsise a whale?

52. Q. What is Jewish Psychiatry?

53. Q. What has killed more Jews than the worst villians of history combined?

(Answers on next page)

ANSWERS

47. A. "Solly wants a Matzoh."

48. A. "Well, just eat the noodles."

49. A. Because the Soviet authorities know they'd never willingly return.

50. A. When a member of the family is sick - or the chicken is.

51. A. You use four skin-divers. (Foreskin divers)

52. A. The care by the Yid of the Odd.

53. A. Jewish cooking.

54. Q. What is the kosher seafood diet?

55. Q. Why is talk so cheap?

56. Q. What is a liberated Jewish woman?

57. Q. What are the two most difficult things in life for a Jew to handle?

58. Q. If you receive this book of riddles as a gift, what is the proper thank you note?

(Answers on next page)

ANSWERS

54.   A. You see food and you eat it.

55.   A. Because supply exceeds demand.

56.   A. One who has sex before her wedding and a job after.

57.   A. Success and failure.

58.   A. Thank you for the book. I'll waste no time reading it.

ISRAEL RIDDLES

1.   Q. What is a Zionist?

2.   Q. How did the United Nations partition of Palestine work out in the end?

3.   Q. How was the land of Israel settled?

4.   Q. How do we know the Arabs really are wholly for peace?

5.   Q. Why in Israel is nobody worried about anti-Semitism?

6.   Q. Why does Israel's finance minister always put on a *yalmulka* (skullcap) before he signs a check?

7.   Q. How does Israel win all its wars?

(Answers on next page)

ANSWERS

1.   A. A Zionist is a Jew who solicits money from a second Jew in order to send to a third Jew to Israel.

2.   A. The Jews got Israel; the Arabs got the United Nations.

3.   A. Yiddle by Yiddle.

4.   A. When it comes to territory, all they want is the whole piece.

5.   A. Because in Israel you had better keep your eyes on the Semites.

6.   A. Because it's the only coverage he has.

7.   A. First all the Jewish doctors are assembled as the first line, then all the Jewish lawyers form the second line, then all the Jewish dentists make up the third line, then the Israeli Officer cries Charge, and you know how they can charge!

8.   Q. What awards do the runners-up in the Mr. Israel contest receive?

9.   Q. Can you jump higher than the Western Wall?

10.   Q. When are Jerusalem's mountains flat, its wadis dry, its streets unpopulated?

11.   Q. When your Israeli taxi loses control going down a steep mountain, what is the first thing you must do?

12.   Q. When the Israeli judge promised to assign the poor defendant a good lawyer, why did he decline the offer?

13.   Q. When two enemy tanks collide in a desert and the Arab cries, "I surrender," what is the appropriate Israeli response?

14.   Q. What is the Jewish blessing for the Syrian army?

(Answers on next page)

ANSWERS

8.   A. Honorable *Menschen*.

9.   A. The Western Wall cannot jump.

10.   A. Whenever you look at the city on a map.

11.   A. Have the driver turn off the meter.

12.   A. The defendant preferred to be assigned a good witness.

13.   A. "Whiplash, whiplash."

14.   A. May the Lord bless and keep them —far away.

15.   Q. Why is it in Israel no one worries about people with concealed weapons?

16.   Q. What is an identity crisis for an Israeli?

17.   Q. How is it that daredevil racing performances are free in Israel?

18.   Q. When given a book on how to cut his work in half, what did the Israeli bureaucrat do?

19.   Q. How is a no smoking sign different in the United States than in Israel?

20.   Q. Which two sports attract fewest Israelis?

21.   Q. In their exchange of military personnel, the United States asked for Generals Dayan, Yadin and Rabin, which Generals did Israel ask for?

(Answers on next page)

ANSWERS

15.   A. In Israel nobody conceals them.

16.   A. When he loses his identity card.

17.   A. They can't charge for looking out your own window.

18.   A. He asked for two copies.

19.   A. In America it means no smoking.

20.   A. Hot-dog skiing in the hills of Haifa and tobogganing in Tel-Aviv.

21.   A. General Electric, General Motors, General Foods.

22.   Q. How come the monument to Israel's unknown soldier is inscribed "Yitzchak Shapiro?"

23.   Q. What was the name of the first luxury liner launched by the Israeli Navy?

24.   Q. What are the safety instructions on El Al Israeli Airlines?

25.   Q. How are bills kept down during Israeli inflation?

26.   Q. How come the Israeli says *shalom* for hello and goodbye?

27.   Q. What is an Israeli bank?

28.   Q. Why were the astronauts' accomplishments so unimpressive to most Israelis?

(Answers on next page)

ANSWERS

22.   A. Because he may have been one of the best known tailors in all of Israel, but as a soldier he was a complete unknown.

23.   A. S.S. Mein Kindt.

24.   A. "Your life vest is under your seat and if you ever need it you should wear it in good health."

25.   A. By a paper weight.

26.   A. With things happening so fast in the Middle East it's hard to know if you're coming or going.

27.   A. A place to keep the money you owe the government until it is asked for.

28.   A. Israelis know that if you have money you can afford to travel.

29.   Q. What is an Israeli bureaucrat doll?

30.   Q. What is especially remarkable about Israeli government bureaucracy?

31.   Q. What is the Jewish underworld called?

32.   Q. How do we know that Theodor Herzl had a great memory?

33.   Q. How do Jewish bank tellers scold their customers?

34.   Q. On which Israeli T.V. program do Tora Readers compete?

35.   Q. Why could Moses our teacher only stutter and stammer?

36.   Q. How many terrorists does it take to celebrate a birthday?

(Answers on next page)

ANSWERS

29.   A. One that winds up but doesn't work.

30.   A. It enables ten men to do the work of one.

31.   A. a) The Cosa Chutzpah.
          b) The Kosher Nostra

32.   A. Because they erected a monument to his memory.

33.   A. You never write, you never call, you only visit when you need money.

34.   A. *Laining* for *Shekels*.

35.   A. He was just learning to cope with Hebrew grammar.

36.   A. 40,001. One to blow out the candles. 40,000 to take the credit.

37.   Q. As a tourist in Cairo, what do you say when you are short changed in the *shuk?*

38.   Q. What is the most popular cigarette in Israel?

39.   Q. In Israel, how do you end up with a small fortune?

40.   Q. What goes zzub, zzub?

41.   Q. Why do Tel-Aviv policemen go around in fours?

42.   Q. How do we know that God loved Israel above all other countries in the world?

43.   Q. What are the two categories of pedestrians in the Tel-Aviv streets?

44.   Q. In the Middle-East, what is peace?

(Answers on next page)

ANSWERS

37.   A. Egypt me!

38.   A. Gefiltered.

39.   A. Come with a large one.

40.   A. A Hebrew speaking bee.

41.   A. One to read, one to count, one to write up the reports and the fourth to keep an eye on the three intellectuals.

42.   A. Why else would he have made the sky blue and white?

43.   A. The quick and the dead.

44.   A. A period of hostility between two periods of fighting.

45.   Q. What are the two evils to be most feared in the Middle-East?

46.   Q. What is the newest, simplified tax form in Israel?

47.   Q. Why in Israel is there no discrimination against the minority?

48.   Q. How do we know that TV in Israel is a poor media?

49.   Q. What is even more difficult than man's never-ending attempt to get to *"know"* the universe?

50.   Q. What is the most imaginative fiction being written in Israel today?

51.   Q. What is it that saves Israel from it's powerful bureaucracy?

(Answers on next page)

ANSWERS

45. A. War and peace.

46. A. How much money did you earn last year? Enclose same.

47. A. In Israel everyone is in the minority.

48. A. Because anything well done is rare.

49. A. Finding you way around downtown Tel-Aviv.

50. A. Income tax returns.

51. A. It's powerful inefficiency.

52. Q. Why do middle-aged Israeli husbands take up jogging?

53. Q. What is the difference between Tel-Aviv and yogurt?

54. Q. Why should Israeli bachelors be heavily taxed?

55. Q. If you should ever need a brain transplant, why is it important to choose an Israeli politician?

56. Q. How do we know Israelis are an even handed people?

57. Q. Why has Israel re-instituted the death penalty?

58. Q. In Israel, what's the difference between death and taxes?

(Answers on next page)

ANSWERS

52.   A. So that they could hear heavy breathing again.

53.   A. Yogurt has an active living culture.

54.   A. It is not fair that some men should be happier than others.

55.   A. You'll want a brain that had never been used.

56.   A. They never speak well of <u>any</u> of their neighbors.

57.   A. Anything to free up another parking place!

58.   A. Death doesn't get worse every time the *knesset* meets.

59. Q. When is it that men and nations in the Middle East begin to act rationally, wisely and sensibly?

60. Q. Why do people keep dogs in Israeli neighborhoods?

61. Q. How do you know you're in a four star restaurant in Tel-Aviv?

62. Q. Who are the normal people living in Tel-Aviv?

63. Q. With the spread of Israeli cities and towns what is the Jerusalemites' greatest fear?

(Answers on next page)

ANSWERS

59. A. When they have exhausted all other alternatives.

60. A. They are usually timid souls lacking the strength of character to bite people themselves.

61. A. You're not required to remove your tray.

62. A. The ones you haven't met yet!

63. A. "Uh, Oh," Here comes Tel-Aviv.

SABBATH AND HOLY DAZE RIDDLES

1.   Q. How do we know that Hitler died on a Jewish holiday?

2.   Q. When does the moon go broke?

3.   Q. How can you tell when the *Shabbat* candle is angry?

4.   Q. Which candles burn longer, the *Shabbat* candles or the *Hanukkah* candles?

5.   Q. What is the best thing to put into the *challah*?

6.   Q. What is the best way of making the *Kugel* of the *Shabbat* meal last?

7.   Q. On what condition was the non-ticket holder permitted to enter the synagogue on the Day of Atonement to deliver a message to a friend?

(Answers on next page)

ANSWERS

1.   A. Any day on which Hitler died would be a Jewish holiday.

2.   A. Just before *Rosh Hodesh*; when it is down to its last quarter.

3.   A. When it flares up.

4.   A. No candles burn longer. They all burn shorter.

5.   A. Teeth.

6.   A.   a) By making the chulent first.
            b) By eating it next week.

7.   A. On the condition that the usher wouldn't catch him praying.

8. Q. Why is it okay to eat oysters on the Jewish holiest fast day?

9. Q. Which day in the calendar are Jews to eat nothing but cured, smoked, herring and salmon?

10. Q. What come at the end of *Yom Kippur?*

11. Q. In connection with the Festival of Tabernacles, what law in the Bible did W.C. Fields make famous?

12. Q. What did the queen say when the nervous Jewish knight forgot his Latin and blurted in Hebrew, *"Ma Nishtana HaLayla Haze?"*

13. Q. Why is *Passover* celebrated by an enormous family meal?

14. Q. In what way is the observance of the *Passover* ritual of opening the door for Elijah different in New York than elsewhere?

(Answers on next page)

ANSWERS

8.   A. There's an R in *Yom Kippur*.

9.   A. *Yom Kipper*.

10.   A. The letter R.

11.   A. Thou shalt never give a *Succah* an even break.

12.   A. "Why is this knight different form all other knights?"

13.   A. So that everyone has a chance to pass over all the delicious food platters to one another.

14.   A. In New York you first must check through the peep-hole to be sure there is no one there.

15.   Q. What must not the Jewish beatnik say on *Passover?*

16.   Q. What category of Jews benefit most from the Rabbi's sermons.

17.   Q. In which direction does the *Passover* wind blow?

18.   Q. How does a Jewish businessman advertise his business in a Christian neighborhood on Easter?

19.   Q. When does *Hanukkah* come before *Sukkot?*

20.   Q. What did the Jewish mother say to her son who was wearing one of the two ties she had given him for *Hanukkah?*

21.   Q. What is the worst thing about eating *Hamentassen* and *Latkes?*

(Answers on next page)

ANSWERS

15. A. "Lay a little bread on me."

16. A. Jewish insomniacs.

17. A. Easterly.

18. A. Jesus may have risen but our prices have not.

19. A. When looking them up in the Jewish Encyclopedia.

20. A. "What's the matter, how come you don't like the other one?"

21. A. Finishing them.

22.   Q. What has no feet or hands but the longer they stand the shorter they grow?

23.   Q. What is the reason we sound the *grogger* on *Purim?*

24.   Q. Did Haman receive his just deserts?

25.   Q. How do we know that the Esther of Jewish history was not a Persian at all, but was a sexy Babylonian?

26.   Q. At the festive meal after the Messiah, why will the Lord serve both meat and fish?

27.   Q. Who comes down the chimney on Hannuka?

28.   Q. What must not an Orthodox Jew say to a Reform Jew if he still wishes to be friends?

(Answers on next page)

ANSWERS

22.   A. The *Hanukkah* candles.

23.   A. To make noise.

24.   A. Yes, he became Hamantashen—just dessert.

25.   A. Because the king called her baby and wouldn't leave her alonia.

26.   A. Fish for those who do not trust His *Kashrut*.

27.   A. The Fiddler on the Roof. It's cold on *Hannuka*.

28.   A. "Now you go forth to worship God in your way and I go to worship God in His."

29. Q. Why on Sabbath do Rabbis offer a piece of their minds?

30. Q. Who more than anyone else worships his creator?

31. Q. In interpreting Jewish law, what is worse than leaning over too far backwards?

32. Q. Why should we not attack God for the world's imperfections?

33. Q. How does Jewish tradition explain death?

34. Q. What did the Saltine say to the Matzoh?

35. Q. Why was little Patrick Rubenstein allowed only half a day from school on Yom Kippur?

(Answers on next page)

ANSWERS

29.   A. Because they have little to lose.

30.   A. A self-made man.

31.   A. Falling flat on your face.

32.   A. He may be as miserable about them as we are.

33.   A. As Nature's way of telling us to slow down.

34.   A. "Funny, you don't look Jewish."

35.   A. He was only half-Jewish.

36.   Q.   What do most Americans think about Hanukkah?

37.   Q.   We know which Jew was born on Christmas. Who was born on Hanukkah?

(Answers on next page)

ANSWERS

36. A. That it is some kind of duck call.

37. A. Hanuk.

RIDDLES FOR THE UNSYNAGOGUED

1.   Q. Marooned on a desert Island, why did the Jew build two synagogues?

2.   Q. Why in the synagogue do we conclude a prayer by saying Amen, and not Awoman?

3.   Q. Why did the elderly Jew's prayer-shawl and prayer-book become water-logged?

4.   Q. How can you take a *kiddush* cup, throw it into the congregation and not spill a drop of wine?

5.   Q. What kind of cheese do you bring to the synagogue?

6.   Q. Is it a greater *mitzvah* for a *torah scribe* to write the torah on an empty stomach or a full stomach?

7.   Q. What are the most popular kinds of Jews after Orthodox, Conservative and Reform?

(Answers on next page)

ANSWERS

1. A. The one to pray in; the other never to set foot in under any circumstances.

2. A. Because the congregation sings Hymns and not Hers.

3. A. Because the doctor told him to take a shower religiously every morning.

4. A. When it is empty.

5. A. Swiss cheese, the holy cheese.

6. A. Neither—a *torah* should be written on parchment.

7. A. Orange and tomato.

8.   Q. How do we know when a Jewish community is especially rich?

9.   Q. Why is it best to come to the synagogue early?

10.   Q. What does the talis say to the *bar-mitzvah*?

11.   Q. Why was the bar-mitzvah given both the bible and an umbrella as a gift from the congregation?

12.   Q. What is the main difference between a ninety-year old rabbi, and a *bar-mitzvah*?

13.   Q. Why during the course of the service is it essential for a *bar-mitzvah* to wear a belt around his waist dividing his body into two equal halves?

14.   Q. Why does the *bar-mitzvah* receive many valuable gifts on his *bar-mitzvah* day?

(Answers on next page)

ANSWERS

8.   A. When they employ a lifeguard for the ritual bath.

9.   A. That way the back seats are not yet gone.

10.   A. You're putting me on.

11.   A. Because they wanted to be sure he'd open at least one of them on occasion.

12.   A. Seventy-seven years.

13.   A. To hold up his pants.

14.   A. Everyone wants him to become a *minyonaire*.

15. Q. Why is the *bar-mitzvah* day so special for the *bar-mitzvah?*

16. Q. What does a Jewish boy become when he is *bar-mitzvah* in China?

17. Q. What belongs to you but is used by others in Hebrew school?

18. Q. Why were the parents of the not-too-bright boy newly enrolled in the Hebrew school advised that the first text he would be taught would be the *Kaddish*—the Jewish prayer for the dead?

19. Q. When dismissed early from Hebrew School, why must you leave quietly?

20. Q. Why could the father no longer help his son with his Hebrew homework?

21. Q. How do we know Columbus was well trained as a *cantor?*

22. Q. Why does the *cantor* go up on the pulpit to chant the *kiddush?*

(Answers on next page)

ANSWERS

15.   A. On that day he becomes one in a *minyon*.

16.   A. He becomes a Man-darin.

17.   A. Your Hebrew name.

18.   A. It was reasoned that by the time he'd get it right he'd probably be needing it.

19.   A. So as not to wake the others.

20.   A. His son had already moved on to the second grade.

21.   A. He was capable of hitting the High Seas.

22.   A. Because no one would hear him if he went <u>under</u> the pulpit to chant the kiddush.

23.   Q. What can the *cantor* break with only his voice?

24.   Q. When does a rabbi become a rabbit?

25.   Q. What do they call the *Mohel* (the ritual circumcisor) from Boston?

26.   Q. In the matter of professional services rendered what distinguishes the rabbi from the *Mohel* (ritual circumcisor)?

27.   Q. At a circumcision, what's the first thing which must traditionally be done when the *Sandek* (Godfather) faints?

28.   Q. Why does the *Mohel* hang out a sign on his window displaying watches and timepieces?

29.   Q. Why aren't there more elephants ordained as rabbis?

(Answers on next page)

ANSWERS

23.   A. Silence.

24.   A. When he has tea.

25.   A. The Yankee Clipper.

26.   A. The rabbi collects fees, the *Mohel*, tips.

27.   A. Make sure to take the baby away from him.

28.   A. What would you rather have him hang out?

29.   A.   a) Because very few elephants finish rabbinical school.
            b) Because there aren't too many Jewish elephants.

30.   Q. Why at services does a rabbi always wear a *yalmulka*?

31.   Q. What do rabbi's wives have that no other wives have?

32.   Q. At what occasion is it permissible for a rabbi to eat ham?

33.   Q. What does it mean in the synagogue when before the sermon, the long-winded rabbi removes his watch and places it before him on the lectern?

34.   Q. What is the difference between marrying a doctor or marrying a rabbi?

35.   Q. If the tailor doesn't charge a rabbi for a suit, what does he get?

36.   Q. Why did Yossie dying of small-pox ask to see a priest?

(Answers on next page)

ANSWERS

30.   A. To cover his head.

31.   A. Rabbi's kids.

32.   A. At a priest's wedding reception.

33.   A. Not a darn thing.

34.   A. The difference is, when you are sick and you are married to a doctor he makes you well for nothing. When you marry a rabbi and you're bad he'll make you good for nothing.

35.   A. A lot of rabbis.

36.   A. He didn't want his rabbi to catch a deadly disease.

37.　Q. When the rabbi of an Orthodox congregation becomes Reform is he de-frocked?

38.　Q. Why do rabbis go on and on with their sermons?

39.　Q. What was the compliment the rabbi received when he first arrived at his new congregation?

40.　Q. Why does one listen to the rabbi?

41.　Q. When the rabbi took ill how did he know his synagogue board really loved him?

42.　Q. What is green, curly and religious?

43.　Q. What would people do if God moved from heaven and lived on earth?

(Answers on next page)

ANSWERS

37. A. No, just un-suited.

38. A. Because shortening is not *kosher*.

39. A. He was told, "Rabbi, we never knew what sin was all about until you came here."

40. A. Because he's got the microphone and you don't.

41. A. Because they voted 10-9 to wish him a speedy recovery.

42. A. Lettuce Pray.

43. A. Break his windows.A rabbi who tells riddles.

44.　Q.　What is a very pious Jew?

45.　Q.　What is the difference between the United Jewish Appeal and Sex Appeal?

46.　Q.　What is the ultimate proof of God's omnipotence?

47.　Q.　How do we know the chicken came before the egg?

48.　Q.　What is even more difficult than becoming a *Tsadik* (saint)?

49.　Q.　What is the difference between Jewish genious and Jewish stupidity?

50.　Q.　Why do some Rabbis get lost in thoughts?

51.　Q.　What must a Rabbi be who tells the truth from the pulpit?

(Answers on next page)

ANSWERS

44.   A.   One who would even be an atheist if his Rabbi was one.

45.   A.   To the former, Jewish women give generously.

46.   A.   That He need not even exist to save us.

47.   A.   It's hard to imagine God sitting on an egg.

48.   A.   Living with one.

49.   A.   Jewish genious has its limits.

50.   A.   Because it is such unfamiliar territory.

51.   A.   A fast packer.

52. Q. Why is life extinct on all other planets of the solar system?

53. Q. What is worse than a *cantor* with a sore throat?

54. Q. Why did the congregation refuse the new *cantor* a *shofar*?

55. Q. Why does the *Mohel* (ritual circumcisor) hang a clock in his window?

56. Q. How is analyzing a rabbi's sermon like dissecting a frog?

57. Q. What is the Golden Rule of synogogue life?

58. Q. How are Rabbis and cats alike?

(Answers on next page)

ANSWERS

52.   A.   Their civilizations were more advanced than ours.

53.   A.   A rabbi who tells riddles.

54.   A.   They figured he could drive himself.

55.   A.   What would you have him hang in his window?

56.   A.   Few people are interested and the frog dies of it.

57.   A.   Whoever has the gold rules.

58.   A.   They both raise Hell but you can't catch them at it.

How do we know that Shloimi was A better batter than Casey at the bat?

SHLOIMI AT THE BAT

The outlook was extremely muddy
for the *Yenimvelt* nine that day;
The score stood two to four,
with but one inning left to play.
So when Hershel popped to shortstop
and Beryl did the same,
A sickly silence fell upon
the *chevra* at the game.

A straggling few got up to go
leaving there the rest,
With the hope which springs eternal
within the human breast.
For they thought: "If only Shloimi
could get a whack at that."
They'd put even money with
big Shloimi at the bat.

But Finkle preceded Shloimi;
likewise the *schnorer* Jake,
And the former was a peddler,
and the latter was a fake.
So on that stricken multitude
grim melancholy sat;
For there seemed but little chance,
of Shloimi getting to bat.

But Finkle let drive a single,
to the wonderment of all.
And the *shlepper* Yonkle tore
the cover off the ball.
And when the dust had lifted,
and they saw what had occurred,
There was Yonkle safe at second,
and Finkle a-hugging third.

Then from the gladdened myriads
there rose a lusty yell;
It rumbled through *Yenimvelt*
it rattled in the dell;
It struck upon the hillside and
rebanked upon the flat;
For there was Shloimi, mighty Shloimi,
advancing to the bat.

There was ease in Shloimi's manner
as he stepped into his place;
There was pride in Shloimi's bearing
and a smile on Shloimi's face;
And when responding to the cheers
he lightly doffed his hat,
No stranger in the crowd could
doubt 'twas big Shloimi at the bat.

Twenty thousand eyes were on him as
he rubbed his hands with dirt,

One thousand *minyans* applauded
when he wiped them on his shirt;
Then when the pitcher began to wind
the ball against his hip,
Defiance gleamed in Shloimi's eye,
a sneer curled Shloimi's lip.

And now the leather-covered sphere
came hurtling through the air,
But Shloimi stood a-watching it
in haughty grandeur there.
Curving by the sturdy batsman,
the ball unheeded sped—
"That ain't my style," muttered Shloimi
"Strike one," the umpire said.

From the benches packed with *lansmen*,
there went up a muffled roar.
Like the beating of the storm waves
on the stern and distant shore.

"Kill him! Kill the umpire!" shouted
some *kleegeh* on the stand;
And its likely they'd have done so
had not Shloimi raised his hand.

With a smile of *Maimonide*an charity
great Shloimi's visage shone;
He stilled the rising tumult,
he bade the game go on;
He signaled to the pitcher,
and once more the spheroid flew;
But Shloimi still ignored it,
and the umpire said, "Strike two!"

"*Gonif!*" cried the maddened *minyans*,
others shouted, "Fraud!"
But one scornful look from Shloimi
and the audience was awed.

They saw his face grow stern and cold,
they saw his muscles strain,
And they knew that Shloimi wouldn't
let the ball go by again.

The sneer is gone from Shloimi's lips,
his teeth are clenched in hate,
He pounds with cruel vengeance
his bat upon the plate;
And now the pitcher holds the ball,
and now he lets it go,
And now the air is shattered
by the force of Shloimi's blow.

Like a rocket in space
to the distant heaven;
Way above heaven six
and far beyond seven;
Past the *cheder* of the *Gaon*
to the seat of the throne
Of the Almighty himself
Mit Got's Helpf:

A black hole round tripper
A four base ripper,
A big bang booming homer,
Is it not stated in tractate *Yoma?*
And before that by
the prophet Jonah?
Not to speak of the *Masorah*
on the "going, going, gona."

A *gezunta* blast
that all the *shreiying* fans may see
It was big Shloimi at the bat—
and not Casey!
Everywhere the sun is shining;
everywhere the *chevra* shout.
There is plentious joy in *Yenimvelt:*
Big Shloimi hit it out.

So much for the telling of this
great baseball thriller
—Now you know
the rest of the *megilla.*

GLOSSARY

cheder	academy
chevra	gang (a group of friends)
Gaon	intellectual authority, dean
gezunta	healthy
gonif	thief
kleegeh	wiseguy
lansman	townsman
Maimonidean	Maimonides was a 12th century philosopher and physician, who defined the Degrees of Charity
Masorah	tradition
megilla	scroll, story
minyan	unit or group of ten
schlepper	ne'er do-well
schnorer	parasite
shreiying	screaming
Yenimvelt	elsewhere (literally, another world)
Yoma	volume of the Talmud
Yonkle	Jake

POSTSCRIPT

The reader may now have come to the correct conclusion that this book which fills a much needed gap could be enormously improved by drastically reducing the space keeping the two covers apart!

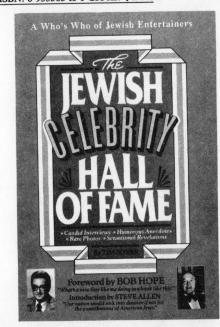